ODYSSEY TO THE UNKNOWN

DISCOVER YOURSELF AS NEVER BEFORE

AYUSH SINHA

I dedicate this book to my mother and my years of
meditation and struggle on the journey I embarked upon
in my earliest boyhood.

Contents

Contents

Preface

This work is an amalgamation of psychology, spirituality, and metaphysics, written in order to point out the simplest truths about meditation and awareness. It reiterates that truth is available to all who can stop and pay attention to the world within and outside, that peace is merely a breath away, and that meditation is the ultimate freedom from inward sorrow.

You are going to cherish the work if you are looking for a complete understanding of meditation, awareness, and the difference between awareness and concentration. The author takes you through a journey he embarked upon in his earliest boyhood after his father's demise, and writes only that which has been witnessed by him in more than 15 years of his quest.

Discover the nuances of meditation and understand by yourself how all of us are meditative in one way or another and that love, meditation, and joy are not three different objectives but the by-products of awareness itself.

Acknowledgements

I owe this work to all the temples, churches, mosques, and gurudwaras I resorted to in my earliest boyhood and to all those who welcomed me there with their warmth without any discrimination. I thank each and every individual I came across on my journey, irrespective of their attitude towards me, since the course of a wave is ascertained by the deepest layers of the Ocean Itself.

All those whose paths crossed mine have so far helped me evolve without fail in one way or another, so Khalil Gibran puts it ineffably, "I have learned silence from the talkative, toleration from the intolerant, and kindness from the unkind; yet strange, I am ungrateful to these teachers."

The poets, philosophers, authors, and mystics I so far feel to have spent my whole boyhood with are Leo Tolstoy, Rabindranath Tagore, Munshi Premchand, Khalil Gibran, Fyodor Dostoevsky, Swami Vivekananda, Jiddu Krishnamurti, Rajneesh Osho, Sandeep Dahiya, Swami Sacchidananda, and Yuval Noah Harari.

I would forever remain indebted to my Mother for being by my side night and day through all my ups and downs. Without her, neither the book nor I would be possible today.

Author's Bio

Ayush Sinha is a lawyer, columnist, communication trainer, and Jyotish - Acharya currently living in New Delhi.

He holds a Bachelor's Degree in Management, a Bachelor's Degree in Law, a Master's Degree in Law, a Master's Degree in Political Science, a Degree equivalent to a Master's Degree in Vedic Astrology, and a Master's Degree in Vedic Astrology, apart from being a research scholar.

He has worked as a Vedic Astrologer, Vastu and Feng Shui Consultant, Numerologist, Palmist, and Meditation Trainer for over a decade now. With thousands of happy clients across the globe, he has had the pleasure of recommending psychology-specific remedies for more than twenty thousand charts.

Walking alone on a secluded path in his earliest boyhood, he encountered numerous miraculous circumstances that led to his realization that truth is independent of all authorities, be they scriptures or organized religions. He leaped out into the world of spirituality merely at the age of eleven, and was shoved by his seclusion not only into the endless world of spirituality and mysticism but also into the world of literature, history, philosophy, and astrology.

Having contributed to more than fifteen anthologies, edited, proofread and translated tens of books, and authored a book as a commentary on the Taittiriya Upanishad, he has been writing for the last thirteen years. He has worked with several national and international news agencies, like Drew Reports News, Republic World and the Times Internet, as an editor and freelance writer.

CHAPTER ONE

WHAT IS MEDITATION?

The understanding of meditation is far more significant than that of how to meditate. Most of us meditate with the notion that meditation is about putting our thoughts to an end, whereas it is about being free from all efforts. The moment we start putting our efforts, meditation comes to an end. However, it is an undeniable fact that some techniques and efforts may be useful at times to take us to the state of meditation, or to a state which renders us capable to meditate.

Gautama was ineffably attractive, with a robust body and enchanting eyes, but meditation had showered nectar upon him. He was once asked by a passer-by in the middle of a forest, "Who are you. Are you a god from heaven?" He shook his head.

"Are you, then, from the court of Indra?"

"No, I am not."

"Are you some Yaksha?"

"No, I am not," the Buddha answered, serenely smiling.

"Are you even a man?" the passer-by asked again, perplexed.

The Buddha again shook his head.

"Are you an animal or bird?"

"No, I am not that either," the Buddha gently answered, leaving the other confused by now

"Who are you, then?"

The Buddha iterated, "I am merely awareness; there is only awareness, only witnessing."

Meditation is merely awareness. It is like sitting on the bank of a river, seeing the constant flow of water. It is seeing things as they are, without clinging to any judgements, opinions, and prejudices. Then, no matter whether we are walking, eating, or sitting, we can be meditative, by being awake, conscious or aware. This is a state of observation without the observer and the object being observed.

Meditation is the flowering of love as it is the very seed of understanding. When we observe, we understand the world within and outside, and this understanding is love and compassion. The understanding as a result of meditation is free from our knowledge since knowledge is a product of the past whereas reality is in the Now.

The past has become the present after modification, and the present is getting modified in front of us to become the future. All the three times—the past, the present, and the future—are one right before us. Thought exists in the realm of the past, as it is a response of memory, and our memory, or our knowledge, is the sum total of all experiences. Therefore, our experiences being limited, our mind, thoughts, and knowledge are limited.

Meditation is the very realization of the limitation of our mind, when we observe all that there is and go beyond it. It is thus the freedom from the body and the mind, when we merely observe both our body and our mind as they are, effortlessly, and realize we are beyond them both like the sky untouched and unaffected by moving clouds of all colours and shapes.

Most of us fail to realize that the nature of the mind is to be chaotic. The mind both creates problems and finds out solutions to them. For instance, the mind that led to the two World Wars came up with the solution of the United Nations. The mind knows neither peace nor awareness and has only distractions of all sorts. It evolves with time and is conditioned differently in different societies.

When we say that a flower is conditioned, we mean to say that certain conditions have come together to bring this flower about. Those conditions may be sunlight, soil, water, air and climate, and in the same way, there are numerous factors behind the structure of our mind. This is the reason why an Indian thinks differently from an American and an American thinks differently from a Chinese. We all think differently because our thoughts are conditioned like our bodies, depending upon the regions we have been brought up in.

The mind, we see, is not a solution but a problem itself. Many a time, it ends up labelling a particular normal situation as a problem as per its own convenience. It calls what we dislike a problem and what we like a solution, so a problem and solution are a matter of our mental states and response in our lives. What is a problem to me may not at all be a problem to you, and what is a solution to you may be a problem to me. If there is heaven within, we can be joyous even in hell, but if there is hell within, we cannot be joyous and thus enjoy even the most wondrous pleasures of heaven. It is plausible that both heaven and hell are within, then.

How to Meditate?

I have often been asked by the curious around how they should meditate, and I have always reiterated that understanding meditation is more important than understanding how to meditate. We need to ask ourselves why we wish to meditate after all. We need to inquire into our very desire to find the supernatural or to meditate. Are we desirous to meditate as an escape from our monotonous, mundane lives?

If we inquire a little, we will get to realize that the only purpose of this life is to live to the fullest. We are all seeking joy, trying to live to the fullest, in one way or another, but rarely do we get to realize that there is great sorrow in our very desire to hold on to life. Nothing in the world being permanent, all that we try to hold on to is bound to fade away sooner or later. When we lose things, we find ourselves sorrowful, and we lose things every second as there is impermanence all around, so we are sorrowful all the while.

We invent hundreds of ways to escape from our sorrow, no matter whether we travel, get into relationships, have sex, watch movies, read books, or become workaholics. Our seeking positivity implies that there is negativity in our lives, and our seeking happiness also means that there is sorrow within us. We keep moving like pendulums throughout our whole lives; running away from disrespect, running after respect; running away from failures, running after success; and running away from what we call death, running after life. When the whole world is rooted in duality—that of light and darkness, men and women, and right and left—we fail to realize that it is impossible to have light without darkness and positivity without negativity. Moreover, running away implies sorrow itself, our running away from what we label 'disrespect, darkness and negativity' and thus dislike. The very movement of running away is sorrow.

The more we run away from something in the world, the more we run after something else. Then, it means, the greater the sorrow within, the stronger the desire to have happiness or an escape from sorrow. Our lives are premised upon running night and day, and when we are running, we can not see what is at front. If we get late for our flight, we ask our drivers to drive fast and find ourselves in a mental state incapable of looking around at the beauty of the road. We can never be one with the world so long as there are self-movements—fear, jealousy, greed, ambition anger, insecurity, lust, and possessiveness.

Understanding the ways of our consciousness—the conscious, the subconscious and the unconscious—is the beginning of meditation. The greatest problem is that human beings are unaware at all levels, and not only at the levels of their mind. It is important and rather practical, then, in this situation that they should get aware step by step, at all levels. We can start with the observation of our body and the ways we move our body parts, sit, eat, drink, and speak. As time passes by, we can move on to the observation of our breathing and how we breathe differently in different mental states. We can see how we breathe differently in anger and sorrow than in excitement and happiness. This is where we get to understand how breathing is deeply connected to our emotions and mental states.

As we get aware of our breathing, we gradually start observing our thoughts themselves. This is where we for the first become aware of the chatter of our minds and the fact that we are beyond our thoughts. As our awareness gets intense here, we become aware of gaps between our thoughts as well, and here comes a state in which there is only our 'beingness or isness'. It is a state of effortlessness. In this state there remains no observer observing thoughts. This state has observation without an observer, and we can say, in the words J Krishnamurti, that the observer becomes the observed here and both of them dissolve. At the same time, the gaps between thoughts become longer and longer as we continue our meditation. That is, the frequency of thoughts starts getting lower and lower.

The above state is that of pure observation, when there is dancing without the dancer, singing without the singer, and love without the lover when both the beloved and the lover are one. This state is that of selflessness and is the door to the unknown world of our consciousness, that is, the subconscious and the unconscious, ninety-five percent of our mind being unconscious. If we here consider thoughts the waves of an ocean, we can call the subconscious and the unconscious the deeper layers of the ocean, and this state is that of awareness of both the waves and the deeper layers—that of the awareness of the whole ocean.

The state of beingness, when we are aware of the body, our breathing and our thoughts, is also where we ask ourselves who we are if all that is there in the mind and the body changes every second. When we were born, we weighed merely around three kilograms and had no thoughts either, and we are so heavy now both psychologically and physiologically. We have of course accumulated both our mind and our body, but who are we, then, beyond our body and mind, beyond all that is permanent?

After we have reached the state of isness, or beingness, I have found out that we become capable of meditation anywhere doing anything, no matter whether we are at a railway station or in a forest or we are walking or sitting. Sitting meditation is required significantly and is indispensable when we are new to meditation, as we are then aware of neither our body nor our mind.

When we are new to meditation, we may need a few efforts and techniques. Some of us are so chaotic that we fail to be aware even of our breathing. When I participated in group meditation in my boyhood, I would meditate for hours every day and find out after a couple of days that a lot of meditators failed to even be simply aware of their inhalation and exhalation. Their minds certainly were more chaotic than those of many others, and as a result, meditation was comparatively difficult for them. In situations like these, where the mind is more chaotic and mechanical than usual, we can start with music, mantra-recitation, or concentration.

Music calms the mind and relaxes and renders the listener capable of the observation of their body and mind. It temporarily breaks the thinking-patterns of our mind and it is one of the reasons why music therapy now has an important place in the world of psychology as well. What we listen to certainly acts upon our mental states strongly. When listening to music is repetitive, the listener gets more and more concentrated and thus capable of entering the world of meditation.

Mantra recitation plays a significant role in calming the mind before actual meditation starts. It is related to concentration and narrows the lane available for the wandering of thoughts. At the same time, every word has certain vibration and is connected to thought itself. If we look deeply into it, we will find out that thought and words are both the same. If the words 'oak tree' are uttered to us, they induce a certain thought often in the form of memory—an image of some oak tree we have seen before. So we can, to a great extent, channelize our wandering thoughts through the chanting of mantras.

When we have all sorts of thoughts replacing one another continually, when we have our thoughts wandering, we find it difficult to observe, that is, to be in a state of meditation. This is where concentration and different techniques available play a paramount role. However, we have to be certain about the fact that these are merely tools required for the preparation for a state of meditation. We have to make sure that we do not cling to any of the techniques as a security.

Here are some of the best ways to concentrate:

1. **Chant a particular mantra for about 30 minutes every day:** We can start with merely 30 minutes every day, and if that, too, seems to be too long for some of us who are more distracted inwardly, we can start with 15 minutes. As time passes by, we will realize that the

duration of our chanting becomes longer and longer. Eventually, we become so concentrated that we find ourselves ready for meditation. That is when we find ourselves capable of observing our thoughts and gaps between them;

2. **Read your favourite books:** Reading, too, is considered part of meditation, for when we read, we observe not only what an author says but what thoughts and ideas occur to us as well. If we read every day for about an hour, we find ourselves capable of meditating in merely 2-3 months. However, many people complain that they fail to read because they find no interest at all. In that case, I suggest that they should read what they like reading, that they should put efforts reading their favourite genres. By and by, they will start reading all genres as their mind gets more and more silent;

3. **Maintain a journal:** Maintaining a journal means observing our thoughts and then putting them into words. The observation of our thoughts, which also means the observation of the functioning of our conscious mind, makes us more and more alert. This at times also puts an end to the wandering of our thoughts. We get to realize the very limitation of our conscious mind, or of our intellect. We get to see how our mind is mechanical and rather repetitive. We thus become aware of the patterns of our thinking as well. This is where we give up thinking and enter the realm of the subconscious;

4. **Listen to music:** When we listen to music and try to be a little observant of our breath, we shift our attention from the outside world to something nearer. Music breaks the patterns of our wandering thoughts. This is where we realize that words strongly induce thinking,

that every word is a thought. Changing the words that enter our head, we change the quality and pattern of our thinking as well. Listening to something new and exotic, at the same time, temporarily puts an end to our thinking, for the old, which is thought, cannot allow or meet the new, which is music. All that we need to be careful about is that the music we listen to must be changed regularly as well to make sure that it does not become old and thus turns out to be a stimulus to thought;

5. **Be more engrossed in your hobbies:** No matter what we like to do, be it reading, writing, eating, cooking, playing, or singing, we can be more involved and absorbed in it. By doing so, we again narrow the lane of our wandering thoughts. We become so absorbed in our activity that most of our thoughts about all our other involvements fade away. Thus, we get a great opportunity here to be observant of our thoughts.

The above ways suggested by me have worked differently for different individuals. It all depended upon the different states of their minds. Some found it easier to read, and for some, music was the best tool to concentrate. The way of an intellectual may be different from that of an artist, but all ways eventually have to lead to the state of isness, or beingness.

We may directly start with the observation of the body and the breath as well if we are comparatively silent, and thus reach a state where we are aware of our body, breath, thoughts, and gaps between thoughts altogether. This state, that of beingness, is where the subconscious and the unconscious unveil themselves, when gaps between thoughts start becoming longer and longer. This is a state when we are purely in the Now, seeing objects, either inside or outside, as they are, without any sort of clinging. This is a state of effortlessness, when we see whatever comes up—of course, as if we were sitting on the bank of a river, seeing the flow of water.

CHAPTER THREE

WHY MEDITATE?

We rarely ask ourselves why we do what we do. We study, learn, earn, procreate and eventually die, and this is what we as humankind have done for hundreds of years. This has become a pattern now and we have become robots programmed by ourselves. Being robots, we can not feel, hear and see the world around. Thus, we can say we have separated ourselves from life and are dead with all our ambitions, fear, jealousy, greed, and insecurities.

Life is ever-changing around, but we have become still by being robotic and mechanical. We have found security in the way of living endorsed by society and this is why almost all our energy is spent merely on conforming to the blueprint laid down by our gurus, religions, psychotherapists, psychologists, scholars, and other authorities. Therefore, the course of our psyche is determined by the outside world and we are guided by our programmed mind in lieu of guiding the mind as a tool.

If we ask humankind why it lives, it will say it does for earning bread, and if we then ask it why it earns bread, it will say that it does to live. This shows the level of illusion within us all. We are all walking like somnambulists, moving in our sleep, and we do not want to wake up either.

Waking up implies going beyond the world of our mind, and our mind then fears its own death. The mind wishes to be active all the while because its very nature is activity and chaos, and not inactivity and stillness.

We need to have a robust understanding of the fact that our mind is limited and that if a cup is full of tea, it is futile as it can contain nothing else. Most of us are night and day so engrossed in our thoughts that we have lost touch with reality unknowingly. Thought, being a response of memory, is always a product of the past, and the past has nothing whatsoever to do with reality as it has changed into the present. Thought thus becomes a deterrent to our being one with reality.

We think we are different both psychologically and physiologically, while the fact is that we are all merely the waves of the same ocean. The differences appear only on the surface and the waves, no matter how large or small they are, are all one deep down.

Sarvam Dukham Sarvam Anityam: There is sorrow all around; there is impermanence all around. Let us go out ask our family members, neighbours, friends, colleagues and acquaintances how happy they are in their lives, and I am sure we are hardly ever going to come across one saying that they again want the same life they are living. Every one of us seems to be suffering in some way or the other, then; some of us through our relationships, some through poor financial conditions and some through poor health.

In the mental state we usually live in, there apparently exist two worlds—the inward world and the outward world. The mind separates itself from the outside world, with its own movements like jealousy, fear, greed, insecurity, possessiveness, lust, and anger. It considers itself a separate entity, as if a wave were separate from the ocean. This in turn results in conflicts between 'them' and 'us'. However, in a state of awareness, when one can observe and thus distance inwardly from all thoughts arising like waves from the mental ocean, there remains no boundary between the outside world and the inward world, that is, both the worlds appear one.

Going deeper into the state of meditation, especially that of 'beingness or isness', we can easily see that thought has created a thinker, with a certain nationality, position, title, caste, and profession, but the moment we get free from thoughts, either by observing them or in sleep, there remains no psychological thinker, and we are then what we observe, or we can say that the observer is the observed.

Thought never lets us see things as they are, nor does it let us be aware, and awareness and thus seeing things as they are implies meditation. Thought is always of the past, and reality is always new, as everything is changing every second. It is only thought at all levels that create distortions in observation.

CHAPTER FOUR

Difference Between Awareness and Concentration

Almost all Indian spiritual schools have emphasized the role of concentration in attaining the state of awareness, while distinguishing between concentration and awareness at the same time. It is unfortunate on the other hand when a majority of us end up confusing one with the other, not going beyond concentration most of the times.

Whereas concentration is a robust tool with an effort to attain awareness for the chaotic, including techniques as to mantras, chanting, and focusing on one point, awareness is effortless. The former is most useful to the more chaotic—to the ones unable to meditate directly. It is an effort to channelize the energy of scattered thoughts, so that thought, instead of having multiple directions, becomes unidirectional.

When most of us have our thought involuntarily directed towards our profession, household affairs, personal life, finance, and so on and so forth, as different forms of anxiety and worries, how great to have our thought unidirectional, that is, directed towards only one object, either in the form of mantras, music, or song? The state of awareness, beyond the clouds of thoughts, is easier to attain from here.

Not everyone is capable to directly be in a state of 'beingness', that is, in a state of 'I am', and concentration serves a great purpose here. Concentration turns out to be a stepping stone to the initial stages of awareness.

We can concentrate through the constant repetition of a particular sound, song, mantra, or stotram. When we concentrate, there is always an effort required, so that our attention has a certain inclusion and exclusion. For instance, when we concentrate on a book, there is an effort to include the content of the book in our attention and exclude any noises around us causing disturbance. An effort is indispensable here, and if there is an effort, it must be from a psychological centre within us, and if there is a centre, there is certainly a division between the subject and the object, or the observer and the object observed. In this case, there is a psychological division between the book and the reader. If we inquire a little seriously and thus meditatively, we will find out that this psychological centre is nothing but one of the manifestations of thought itself at the conscious level of our mind.

Thought has created a thinker, or a centre, who is a reader, writer, astrologist, or spiritualist, with a certain past; the past here is the thinker or centre themself. This past, with all the experiences as its base, experience the present, and thus, there is always a distortion in observation. One from Southern India, with one's past experiences, may not like the lifestyle of North India, calling it superficial, and this observation, that the lifestyle is superficial, is dependent upon one's experiences. As we can see, concentration requires efforts and leads to distorted observation.

Awareness is beyond concentration and is effortless, and this is what we call meditation. It is to be in the Now. Let us have a look at how it functions in view of observation and the role of thought.

Suppose one comes across an old friend who once slapped one years ago. While the latter may have changed and become a saint, everything changing every second, one's mind says that it is the same old enemy and thus a criminal. One is deeply stuck to the past in the form of a thought in the form of an image of the latter having been a criminal. Whereas the past, having got modified, has become the present, one looks upon the past as the reality here. This is where observation is distorted.

In a state of awareness, one would have observed both the thought in the form of the image of having been slapped by that friend, and that friend themselves. It is the observation of both the man and the thought within, so that there remains no division between the outside world and the inside world. It is complete observation, as it were—pure observation. It has no distortion at all, if one is completely aware.

Thought says nothing change, as it is the past, and the past is the dead, whereas awareness implies being one with impermanence. Awareness therefore goes beyond death and birth. Of course, we must be beyond what we can observe. If we can observe the cell-phones we hold in our hands, we must not be our cell-phones, and if we can observe our body and mind, we must be beyond them both.

Awareness, as is clear, is without a centre, since it is beyond thought, while concentration has a centre. Awareness is effortless as all efforts are put by the mind, but concentration involves efforts.

Below is a chart for a clear distinction between awareness and concentration:

Awareness	Concentration
It is beyond thoughts.	It involves thoughts.
It is effortless.	It requires efforts.
It is the observation of all thoughts that appear while observing the Now.	It is an act of including one object to be focused upon and excluding other objects.
It involves wholistic or pure observation.	It involves a somewhat distorted observation.
Thought does not act as a screen in observation.	Thought acts as a screen in observation here.
It is beyond concentration.	It is a stepping stone to awareness.

Difference Between Concentration and Awareness

CHAPTER FIVE

WHY DO WE HAVE DIFFERENT TECHNIQUES FOR MEDITATION?

We are all different with our different ways of conditioning, and thus if Bhakti Yoga or Gyan Yoga suits one, Raj Yoga or Karma Yoga may suit to another. There may be different streams of a river, but the river, with all its streams, have only one end—the ocean. The end of all these Yogas or the different techniques we have for meditation is awareness.

Most of us at the beginning of our spiritual practice also try to impose our techniques over other beginners, thinking that our techniques must be the most powerful. Years ago I was working with a doctor from the United States of America, having migrated from India; his technique was Kriya Yoga, and he had a great issue with another technique of meditation called Vipassana. I found out that while he had distorted and clung to his technique, he had developed biases against other techniques of meditation. His progress had stopped as the technique had become more important than awareness. Unfortunately, this is what happens to most of us beginning to practise meditation.

Most of us have turned the art of meditation complex while the art of meditation is the art of living. It is as natural as breathing, and we can meditate while sitting on a bench in woods or bus, walking, eating, or even sleeping. It is to be one with all that there is; it is to be in the Now, for the reality is in the Now.

Different people endowed with different sorts of intelligence may take help from different paths and techniques. A layman with no intellectual inclination can take up the path of Bhakti Yoga as easily as a scholar can take up Gyan Yoga or a politician can take up Karma Yoga. The end result, however, must be awareness for all these techniques and paths. No scholar must impose Gyan Yoga or Raj Yoga on a peasant who can easily attain awareness through Bhakti Yoga.

The way of Meera and Ramakrishna Paramhamsa must be different from that of Jiddu Krishnamurti and Raman Maharshi, and this is something we Indians have understood better than others in the world. That is why have had different personal gods while the Upanishads have professed **Satyam Gyanam Anantam Brahman**—Truth, Awareness, and Eternity being Brahman. It has for aeons remained a culture with both monotheism and polytheism, since our seers had a robust understanding that different individuals must have different qualities of intelligence.

We also see that Bhakti Yoga, Gyan Yoga, Raj Yoga and Karma Yoga are all interconnected. With a rise in awareness, all of them come about together. We become a Bhakt with our open eyes, with respect for everything and everyone in life; we attain knowledge with an open and empty mind; we practise meditation as part of Raj Yoga as a natural process while doing any activity; and we perform karmas with no desire for fruits. Awareness is all-inclusive.

All that we can be a little careful about is not clinging to any technique on the path of spirituality, otherwise instead of being one with impermanence, we will end up hallucinating for the permanence of our technique itself. This is where most of us end up being mechanical and our growth thus stops. We end up getting stuck in our own webs.

The Buddha beautiful put it, "After having crossed a river through a boat, we cannot end up carrying the boat on our head."

CHAPTER SIX

DIFFERENCE BETWEEN RELIGION AND SPIRITUALITY

"If you want to be religious, enter not the gate of any organized religions. They do a hundred times more evil than good, because they stop the growth of each one's individual development," said Swami Vivekananda, in a speech delivered in San Francisco, on May 29, 1900. He wonderfully cast light on the danger beliefs, through organized religions, bring about in society. One needn't believe in what one has witnessed out of awareness, so there is no question whatsoever of believing or disbelieving in truth. Every believer or disbeliever is thus deterred from experiencing the wonders of the Universe, and their mind is eventually dulled by fears and greed.

The world has been ravaged on and on by various wars and tyrannies so far and a lot of them were premised only upon religious beliefs. Today as well, we talk about communal frictions being the greatest cause of the disintegration of many nations in the past and future. When the belief of one community is different from that of another, there are bound to be conflicts and bloodsheds, and beliefs are inevitable without the psychological evolution required to see things as they are.

Suppose we are in a locked room with no sunlight entering it, there is no way to get to know if the sun is out, and someone all of a sudden enters the room and says that the day is pretty sunny. We have no option other that of believing them. It is because we cannot see by ourselves if the sun is indeed out. Thus, as we see, beliefs become indispensable when we find ourselves incapable to be one with reality or when we are too lazy to inquire.

Yesterday I was discussing with one of my friends the reason behind YouTubers and social media influencers being so prominent and reliable to the majority today. Whereas she found it normal, I wanted to dig deeper about these influencers always eager to quote different scriptures and individuals. I asked her thus if the description of the Himalayas is the actual Himalayas.

Of course, the description of the Himalayas is not the Himalayas at all as it has now snow in it. At the same time, the description is useless once we have reached the Himalayas. That is, truth cannot be monopolized by a scripture, guru, religion, or book. Truth, which is the existential, like sunlight or wind, is available to us all, and what has been observed by someone else can be observed by us as well.

Whereas religion is a codification of truths, spirituality means direct experience, or *Shuddh Anubhuti*. The latter implies pure observation as a result of awareness. We can also say that spirituality itself is the source of all religions in the world.

Organized religions served a great purpose in the world at a point of time of evolution, when the world throughout needed orders to work, but it seems to be high time now that we should all move towards spirituality, that is, direct experience, from wherever we are.

CHAPTER SEVEN

No, We Are Not Different In Any Way

When a flower is called conditioned by us, we imply that certain conditions have come together to bring it about—conditions like sunlight, weather, soil, air, and water. That means long before it bloomed, it was existent in clouds, rivers, air, land, and the sun, that it will continue to exist even after it has withered away completely. In the same way, humans have been conditioned, both psychologically and physiologically, for years by their demography, religions, cultures, traditions, tribes, and families. Like that of the flower, the existence of humans, too, is out of the question without these conditions.

When we were born, we weighed merely around 3 kilograms, without any thoughts about anything going on around us, and years after our birth today, we are many times heavier both psychologically and physiologically. We have ostensibly accumulated a lot from our surroundings, or we can say that we, like that flower, is made of the conditions around us—conditions like politics, religions, nationalities, cultures, traditions, and castes. We are those conditions themselves, as it were, which have evolved for centuries, and our opinions, choices, inclinations, and idiosyncrasies are thus borrowed and not ours at all.

Surprisingly, our conditioning is so strong that the very fact that our thoughts and the way we think are both impersonal is unacceptable to us. We hold a certain level of pride in calling ourselves independent and thus different from the rest of the world. How else can we put ourselves on a pedestal, running away from the horrifying gloom of our mundane life? Though waves of the same ocean, we are compelled to think that we are different, since waves appear separate on the surface with different names and forms. We fail to see how our ancestors are still alive in each and every cell of our body and how we carry all those within us who have ever affected us in any way.

We go on running after light, running away from darkness; running after success, running away from failures; and running after respect, running away from disrespect. Running day in, day out, we fail to be one with all that is before us—life itself. Devoid of love for life, we move to professional stability and success; sick of monotony in our professional life, we move to relationships, marriage and children; out of boredom in our both professional and personal lives, we seek the supernatural. We go on running, and life, hidden behind the veil of illusions, is left behind. While life keeps knocking at our door, we keep wandering from place to place in our city in search of it.

Since we are the products of millions of years of evolution, we carry the sorrow of the whole world, through all that humankind has gone through so far—all the wars, famines, catastrophes, and large-scale events. It is something shared by us all across the globe through collective consciousness, or what some psychologists call the *group-mind*. This collective consciousness, which is the deeper layers of the mental ocean, is the very source of our individual consciousness, which appears personal in nature, and is merely waves on the surface of the mental ocean, with all our personal, professional, and social relationships. Let us try to understand it with the following example. The monthly budget of our family must be dependent upon the economy of the world and our country. If the former is considered individual consciousness, the latter is collective consciousness, both of them being the different layers of the same ocean.

Dependent on time, modifying night and day, we have different layers of human consciousness, but the question is, what is at the end of all the layers, all that is beyond time? Any object limited in space, like our bodies, must be dependent on time, changing every second. So should that which is independent of time, unchangeable in all ways, be beyond space itself, omnipresent and inexplicable?

It is beautiful to be aware of the intelligence behind the interconnection and interdependence of all seemingly different and separate objects in the universe. The immense cosmic intelligence behind the clouds hovering over us, birds chirping in the vastness of the sky, trees dancing to gentle gusts of wind, and sun rising and setting every day, is far beyond our petty thinking. It is untouched by the order put together by the human mind but seems to be behind all the orders in the world. Without the earth, there would be no humans; without the sun, there would be no life on the earth; and without the galaxy, there would be no star called the *sun* either. We all are one here, thus, without any separate existence, us being the whole world.

Interacting with an acquaintance one day, I found out that there is an inherent tendency within us to discard all that is beyond the realm of the mind. The mind finds itself uncomfortable and sometimes even incapable to get in touch with all that it has never experienced before, for going beyond the known for it implies going beyond itself. This sounds paradoxical, hitherto, since going beyond the mind means dropping off the mind itself.

The mind serves as a computer, laden with software and hardware, full of memories, experiences, prejudices, thoughts and judgements. The greater the age of an individual, thus, the more difficult it is to mould the mind, as a cup that is full of tea has no room for even a bit of juice. This is where we realize how a preoccupied mind is equivalent to garbage and is a great deterrent to creativity, when creativity means to bring about something new and the whole structure of the mind is old.

Numerous ideologies, like communism, capitalism, socialism, chauvinism, nationalism and so on and so forth, have impacted the progress of humankind for hundreds of years. We have witnessed them all rising like giant waves in the tempests of the ocean of intellect and subsiding soon thereafter with almost the same momentum. They have all left their legacy behind, either positively or negatively, and we cannot deny the fact that we are influenced by them so far. In fact, the whole history of humankind resides in our collective consciousness.

One has greed, fear, jealousy, insecurity, possessiveness and anger, so has another, and so have all the individuals of this world. This is evidential of how we share a significantly major portion of our consciousness, called by many psychologists now 'collective consciousness'. Though one may be greedy for a lakh rupees and another for ten lakh rupees, greed is common to the consciousness of both; in the same way, one may be fearful of failing an exam and another of poverty, but fear is common to the consciousness of both. Now the question is, what comes before? Is it collective consciousness, which is fear, or individual consciousness, which is fear of poverty?

The waves appear different on the surface of an ocean, but deep down, they are all one—the ocean itself. Ostensibly, the surface of a lake exists only because of the deeper layers of the lake, so individual consciousness must exist only because of collective consciousness, also called 'group consciousness'. It is plausible that fear must have existed far earlier than a specific fear like that of poverty or failing an examination, that greed must have preceded a specific one like one for money or fame.

The monthly budget of an individual must depend upon the economy of their country. If a middle-class family of three members in India requires at least 30 thousand rupees per month to survive comfortably in a tier-3 city, a similar family in Pakistan may require 1 lakh rupees to survive the same way. It is all owing to the differences in the economies of both the countries, again indicating the currency-value, manufacturing capability, gross domestic product, and imports and exports. As is apparent, the economic condition within a house is subservient to the economic condition of something eternally larger being the country. If we consider the family budget individual consciousness, the country's economy is for sure collective consciousness, the latter shaping the former, the former being dependent on the latter.

We have been programmed to believe that there exists nothing like collective consciousness at all, and that we are all independent both psychologically and physiologically. As a result, we have always taken our ideologies, religious inclinations, beliefs, and numerous intellectual schools too seriously. When we were born, we weighed about two and a half kilograms and were devoid of all sorts of thoughts, ideologies, prejudices and inclinations, but now that we have grown significantly through so many years, we have accumulated enough from around. We are now cups full of refreshing, alluring tea, but we seem to have no space for anything else like juice or coffee. It seems we are second-hand human beings with great skills of painting upon us, adding a sense of newness and originality.

CHAPTER EIGHT

WHY ARE WE OBSESSED WITH IDENTIFICATIONS?

I am not sure if we ever wonder how obsessed we often are with our identifications and if there exists any part of us beyond these identifications as well. I mean, even in a beautifully diverse country like India, there are so many identifications, like Brahmins, Kshatriyas, Vaishyas, Shudras, Dravidians, Aryans, North Indians, South Indians, and many others based upon castes, creeds, languages and a lot more. What is Mr. A after all? Remove from him his caste, creed, nationality, family lineage, bank balance, degrees, erudition, social circle, and all that he defines himself through. What is left of him? What is Mr. A behind these identifications that he thinks he is? So, the famous philosopher Descartes proclaims, "I think, therefore I am," but my question, "Who am I when I do not think?"

Just like everything existential, these identifications do serve a purpose by creating around us a safety valve, and this is how we feel safer, stronger and more secure amid our evolution that favours natural selection. However, if left uncontrolled, our identifications are bound to become the sole reason behind a more struggleful, sometimes delayed, and animalistic evolution of humans. Not only that, the identifications deter us from being one with the world as well: we keep running after them like the traffic police instead of sitting at the steps of our courtyards to enjoy the convoy of beautiful vehicles possessed and driven by strangers on the road.

The only way to be secure is to be one with all insecurities, since all that we cling to in search of security is bound to create more and more insecurities because nothing at all is static in the world, everything changing every second. Clinging to anything inside or outside can never bring security in our lives, and when we hold on to our identifications—degrees, bank balance, creed, nationality, caste, social circle, and relations—we create more and more insecurities and this in turn implies a greater sorrow for us. It is ostensible that there is absolutely no way to be joyous and exuberant with much clinging to so many identities, and someone thus puts it so well, "If you have to go far, you must be light enough," Indeed, we cannot move far on this journey with a heavy burden on our heads; we must travel light.

CHAPTER NINE

PRARABDHA: THE INEVITABLE OFFSPRING OF DESTINY AND FREE WILL

Ravana, the erudite mythological king of the Lanka Nagari, found himself perturbed by the prospect of Shani in the 12th house at the time of his son Indrajeet's birth. Shani in the 12th house could have resulted in his son's life outside Lanka and a strained paternal relationship. Thus, the mighty king, blessed with numerous siddhis, found it best to pull Shani back to the 11th house and eventually break his leg as well.

Indrajeet, one who defeated even Indra, the King of Devas, grew up to be an exceptional warrior with the same pride and pomp as his scholarly father. Shani in the 11th house of his birth-chart turned him into a great statesman, but unfortunately at the cost of his humility and spiritual wisdom. We all know about his end through Rama in the battlefield of the Ramayana, the same position of Shani also having contributed to his disturbed relationship with his uncle, Vibhishana.

Does it not seem that Ravana's own Prarabdha forced him to pull Shani back to the 11th house, thus leading to the end of his own lineage, despite the fact that he wanted the best for his son?

In our Shashtras, Prarabdha is said to be the results of previous activities that have already begun to bear fruits in the form of happiness and distress. It is those karmic tendencies of ours whose results are bound to manifest in our lives. These results therefore must be irrefutable, unchangeable and inevitable, like our blood groups, family members, longevity, death and birth. This is also indicative of ourselves being the only causes of our sorrow and happiness and of all the events of our lives. The past, having got modified, has become the present, and the present, getting modified in the Now, is becoming the future.

Suppose an individual in a city walks to a usually secluded crossroad at 05:05:05 PM and a bus runs over him as soon as reaches there. There are numerous questions to be asked:

1. Why did only he, among thousands of individuals in the city, go to that crossroad? Anyone else could have been in his place.
2. Why did the bus driver make the mistake the moment the individual reached the crossroad?
3. Why did the individual go to only that crossroad in a city with hundreds of other crossroads?
4. Most significantly, why did the individual go to the crossroad exactly at 05:05:05 PM?

In some layer of his mental ocean, that is, in his unconscious mind, there must have been some karmic tendency that led him to that crossroad exactly at 05:05:05 PM. It was his own consciousness therefore that forced him to the circumstance. Undoubtedly, it is we ourselves who are the only cause of our sorrow and happiness—no one else.

Nishaad-Raaj Guha, Rama's friend, asked him how the latter would be able to walk without his Padukas or Khadaus (wooden footwear) and Rama shared about his boyhood training under Guru Vashishta for living in forests, adding that his Guru was aware of what was coming up for him. The inquisitive king of Nishaadas again asked if his Guru could not change anything if he had foreseen Rama's exile. Rama smilingly answered, "No one could change; and no one can be free from the fetters of karmas, my friend—not even Devas."

Kaikeyi, who could never have thought of discriminating between Rama and Bharata, all of a sudden lost herself to the insolence of fate. Her desire for Bharata, in lieu of Rama, to be crowned as the King of Ajodhya, turned out to be the sole reason behind the Ramayana. Rama happily accepted it as his Prarabdha, aware of it all to be for the best for the fate of humankind.

What needs to be understood here is that we are the sole reason behind all our happiness and sorrow, and that we choose our happiness or sorrow either consciously or unconsciously. I am reminded of a great instance from my past, about ten years ago. One day, one of my friends came up to me with a confusion about two proposals for his marriage. The first girl was a doctor, whereas the other did nothing and preferred to be a housewife. Though my friend appeared to be confused about the better between the two,

I knew he inwardly was bound to choose who he was going to choose and that he was just unaware of and unconscious about the same.

I got my friend two options. First, that of marrying the doctor, being free from financial responsibilities after marriage, and expecting less time for romance in his personal life. Second, that of marrying the other who preferred to be a housewife, supporting her financially, and having a far better romance life. Not surprisingly enough, he chose the doctor, and I knew he would, since he had struggled with finances all his life and wanted no more financial liabilities or burdens.

Ten years after his marriage, he visited me again with a long face with far less laughter, ranting about his wife rarely having had time for his or for their child's care. He felt deprived of love and blamed his wife. All I asked him was this: "Didn't only you choose to marry a doctor, when you had two options?"

Only the deeper layers of our consciousness compel us to choose our happiness or sorrow, thus choosing all the people and events of our lives. Only we create our lives, and no one else.

CHAPTER TEN

THE ROLE AND LIMITATION OF THOUGHT

A few days ago, I came across a woman zealously talking about self-love. She seemed to have been greatly influenced by influencers from Instagram. However, it was not at all surprising to me when I got nothing but exasperated silence in response to my question as to what the self was. She must have thought me a great idiot! I loved it, though, as always.

It is an era of influencers and books and independent self-inquiry seem to have taken a backseat for the time being. The majority of us with a retrospectively short attention-span find it more convenient to grasp titbits here and there on social media. Strenuous, and rather unreasonable, it appears to us, then, to be in seclusion to go through voluminous books authored by some of the most intelligent individuals of the last two millenniums. Not to forget, influencers' videos we watch must be as short as possible, and the same is taken care of in the subtlest way.

It may be undeniable that all of us have different levels of intellect depending upon psychological evolution which further depends upon a lot of external and internal factors. When a particular content is created for the majority of us, it must be aimed at us in such a way that its information is easily, effortlessly grasped by most of us as well. Therefore, the content produced thus must be average, or at times mediocre, and this is the best in the interests of influencers.

Growing up as a teenager, I always wondered why any authors read by a majority failed to appeal to me as much as the most perspicacious authors a handful of people had heard of. As a result, I ended up reading Fyodor Dostoevsky, Nikolai Gogol, Ernest Hemingway, Munshi Premchand, Leo Tolstoy, and Thoreau. I had at an early age realized that the priceless can never be available to a majority, that that which is for a majority must be mediocrity.

Though I am rarely ever active on social media, I have recently come across a podcast produced by a young man famous in India as a star-YouTuber. The production started with his opinions about Hanuman Chalisa and meditation and ended with the importance of prayer and the fulfilment of desires and thus greed. I could see thousands of comments appreciating the messiah for enlightening the public in a go. With a range of topics, from politics and sex to meditation and the methods to pray, he has millions of online followers, by the way, with a couple of dark circles below his eyes proving his sleep-depravity and sexuality causing ineffable joy always shared with the majority.

When most of us stand on the shore of mediocrity and possess mediocre intellect, the content created for the majority must be mediocre as well. This is why influencers with the greatest number of followers must try to blurt out only that which appeals to the intellect of the majority. In this case, either the most confused end up turning into star-influencers, the most confused and mediocre end up following influencers, or the most mediocre content is produced.

Those with the utmost strength among us must be complacent about following any individual, either inwardly or outwardly. They must be free from all authorities to see things as they are, with the desire to have no limelight whatsoever. Those ready to die and living for truth, to be one with life and the world, can never be into self-gratification, like some reducing psychology to merely psychotherapy as a tool. Truth to them will then be both the means and the end.

We are always full of words-God, love, comfort, relationship, hope-in spite of a conspicuous fact that a word is not the actual object. The word sun is not the actual sun, as the word is but a product of thought, and the thought about the sun has nothing whatsoever to do with the existence of the actual sun. One is one with the sun only when one goes out and stands in its light, and not when one is thinking of the sun in a locked room full of darkness. Therefore, the more full of thoughts and words we are, the more out of touch with reality, as thought, which is a product of the past, is not the reality before us.

The woman was startled by the question of the poor chap and wanted to go no farther. Perhaps she was seeking something else-some kind of validation. What could a man devoid of intellect and words give a woman full of intellect and words? Intellectuals, like her, stand on a rare pedestal far away from simple, ordinary men and women like you and me.

Thought has created a thinker, that is, a centre or self, who belongs to a certain community, nationality, or creed, with certain experiences and achievements. We may say that we are great writers, poets, painters and artists, with wonderful experiences and robust bank-accounts, so we are different centres or selves created by thought. It must be clear to us that there are no centres or thinkers if there is no thought - either in awareness or deep sleep. As long as there is thought, there is a past, and this past is the centre or the self, with its own movements of greed, jealousy, ambition, fear, insecurity, aggression, and anger. The moment one is free from thought, or the past, one is free from the movements, too, as a result of the dissolution of the self.

Thought has created a duality which breeds but conflicts. You and I, who are two different centres created by thought, come across each other and it results in conflicts. Thus, there are conflicts between a Pakistani and an Indian, between a Hindu and a Muslim, and between the West and the East. It is plausible that conflicts are not outside on the borders but within all of us. So, what needs to be transformed is our own consciousness, us creating nations - a wave being the whole ocean.

Years ago, I chanced upon an aged renunciate living in Vadodara, hailing from the ancient city of Ujjain. Deeply immersed in the wonders of spirituality and the occult in my early boyhood, I easily mingled with him as well and we soon started talking almost every week. He was in his early sixties, unmarried, and I put the so-called religious essence of chastity on a pedestal then.

Though he possessed all the luxuries the majority of our countrymen merely dreamt of, I was also unaware of his desire to have a conjugal companion for the rest of his life.

By and by, I saw his desire getting stronger and stronger, and it distanced me. I had already concluded that there had been no fragrance of love or selflessness in his life, until I got to know that the same renunciate had brought up about fifty orphans before his renunciation.

Perplexed, I asked myself, then, which side of the renunciate could be considered his. The side before the renunciation or the side after? It was enough for the realization that we perceive only that which we wish to perceive, out of our insecurities, fear, jealousy, greed, ambition, and anger. Every one of us has two sides, and thus, what we choose to see is up to us.

Let us again have a glance at how thought takes us away from reality and thus creates a duality. Here is an excerpt from one of my old articles, entitled The Limitation of Thought:

"Thought, which is a response of memory, is always a product of the past, and the past has nothing whatsoever to do with reality as it has changed into the present. Everything changing every second, what was a reality yesterday is no longer a reality today; thus, thought starts acting as a deterrent to the wholistic observation of all that is existential in the present, saying that nothing has changed at all.

We must also be certain about the fact that there exist no past, present, and future at all: all that there is, is in the Now. The past has got modified and become the present, and the present, getting modified right before us, is becoming the future. All the three times, then, are inseparable and one, constant change being all around."

There is pure observation only when one observes both thoughts and the objects outside, not when one goes on thinking intensely. Thinking intensely only takes one away from what is right in front of one. On the other hand, one is not in the Now only in the Now; that one has lost touch with reality is reality itself. So, to be one with reality, to be in the Now, one has to be one with one's not being one with reality, that is, one needs to observe one's thinking itself. Thereafter, one is effortlessly free from the centre, and in this freedom, there remains no duality either. The observer becomes the objects being observed. This is the essence of true meditation, and this is self-discovery. One can do it either by sitting, walking, travelling, or romancing.

As one meditates, the deep layers of the mental ocean come up, that is, the unconscious comes up and becomes the conscious. As a result, one is freed from the unconscious mental tendencies as well. It is the process of knowing thyself and the Ultimate Freedom.

Do you know what divides you from me, mate?
That which is absent in that thoughtless state,
When we become what is before our eyes,
When we are the dawn, the sun, and the sunrise.
There is no self, nor its movement, then,
Nor is there any past, any scriptures, or religion;
There is no place for fanaticism or distress,
When this duality itself turns into oneness.
The love growing in the light of timelessness,
The light that has no judgement or selfishness,
It is in that love that we are one with one another,
Let that love grow, my mate, let that love grow forever.

CHAPTER ELEVEN

WHY ARE WE NOT CURIOUS?

Humankind seems to have come a long way today, from the point of the discovery of fire to urbanization, industrialization and the scientific revolution. Hunter-gatherers with long teeth, small brains, and large bodies have now evolved into beings talking about religions, spirituality, and climate change. Not only do they now have clothes crafted to cover their bodies attractively and tantalizingly but they also have hundreds of psychological masks to veil their real animalistic characters.

After the discovery of fire, evolution seems to have pushed our ancestors with shorter teeth into agriculture, and agriculture required permanent settlement, which further led to the formation of tribes. Our ancestors soon had villages and their politics premised upon the dominance of the economically, socially and psychologically privileged. Thus, it was the beginning of the monopolization of what we call the culture and tradition meant for the superior in society. It was the beginning of induced inequality, dominance and discrimination.

Our lifestyles may have vastly changed, then, but the instinct we have inherited from our ancestors manifests itself every now and then in our lives. Our struggle for survival, the desire for eternal riches, workplace politics and toxicity, domestic violence, our pumping our curves out of our inferiority complexes, our sexual tendencies, all of them are redolent of alpha males and alpha females among our ancestors, thousands of years ago, be they Homo Neanderthals, Denisovans, or Orangutans.

Though the potion remains the same, the bottle has conspicuously changed. It is certain that we have successfully invented countless ways to hide our animalism—our ideologies like liberalism, rightism, leftism, or socialism or our so-called superior cultures and traditions.

If we go to Northern India, we come across a huge population interested in civil services for various reasons, some of them being lack of good opportunities, poverty, struggle due to overpopulation, and lack of inclinations to the fields of art, science, spirituality, and literature. All the reasons are interconnected, and of course, none can think of pursuing literature and art amid deep poverty. Due to complete isolation, socially, financially, and educationally, some areas and their population remain indignant and indifferent to the very fact of the oneness and endlessness of the universe and individualistic possibilities. In situations like these, education merely turns out to be a tool meant to be thrown away as soon as it has served its purpose. It eventually slows down the very psychological development of an individual.

The majority of the Indian Subcontinent appears prosperous in history, but there was a time when education was available only to a minority, especially to communities traditionally involved in literary, administrative or religious pursuits. This meant that the rest of the population had people with different occupations, like those of business, agriculture, peasantry and craftsmanship. The role of evolution seemed to wait for the complete destruction of the communal divisions Indians had created in view of different occupations. Moreover, history awaited a time when education would be important and available to all, and it paved the way for a society free from the divisions of castes, creeds and cultures.

Upward social mobility went on, and education became paramount to all, but unfortunately, the subconscious, or the deeper layers of the mental ocean, still had differences. The subconscious of one from a business community appeared different from that of another from a scribal community. As was apparent, it would take many years for all to be similarly inclined, as their conscious minds were newly modified with their subconscious still carrying different old tendencies, premised upon collective consciousness. However, it was all the advent of today's neo-middle-class of the Indian subcontinent.

It is a wonderful sight indeed for us all today to see the majority of us standing on the same pedestal. After all, it is hundreds of years of struggle of the most evolved of this land, be they social revolutionaries, scientists, spiritualists, writers, or the enlightened. The future certainly promises far better days for humankind in the lore of evolution.

CHAPTER TWELVE

ARE WE ONE WITH LIFE?

Throughout our whole lives, we run after our dreams, in search of our favorite destinations. These runs also give us a sense of busyness, thus getting us completely focused on whatever we want to have in our futures, taking us away from the beauty of our journeys. Of course, when we day in, day out think of whatever we want to have in the future, we are bound to miss whatever we already have before us in the present. We miss to be one with the beauty of the clouds hovering over our heads, of the birds chirping in the vastness of the sky, of the trees dancing to a soothing breeze.

There comes a point in everyone's life where they realize that there is no destination at all and that there are only journeys in this life. This is the point where a mind conditioned by society starts opening to the grand truth that every end is a new beginning, that every creation is a destruction, that there can be no creation without destruction at all. Life seems to be a flux, then, creation and destruction being the same, everything, including our own selves, being impermanent in the world. Thus, here comes the question we seldom ask ourselves amidst our busyness, what do we stick to when nothing is still or permanent at all? The moment we stick to something, or the moment we try to cage something, it disappears. There comes about an ineffable sense of insecurity then, with the fear of losing whatever we hold on to the most. We yearn for what we don't have, but after acquiring it, we just fear losing it.

We dream of getting fame, success, money, and whatever else allures us, but our camouflage doesn't let us see that only in those dreams of ours is something that seems great to us. We imagine ourselves getting in the future whatever we lack today, and in this imagination, we get a great pleasure. However, after acquiring whatever we dream of, we cease to imagine, for we don't need to imagine whatever is before us in the present. The very cessation means the end of our pleasures we get while imagining ourselves acquiring whatever we want to have. Therefore, here begins a game at the unconscious levels of our minds. We again start searching for new destinations to please ourselves, which becomes an endless race, of hundreds of new travails, sacrifices, and sorrows.

The whole of this life is impermanence, everything changing every second here, and nothing can be stopped from disappearing. It is we who should therefore ask ourselves why we fail to free ourselves from the cage of our societal programming, as to why we fail to be one with the beauty of impermanence. We suffer not because there is change and uncertainty all around but because we want security, when insecurity is the only security in the world. We suffer not because there is impermanence all around but because we want our favorite things to be permanent, when impermanence is the only thing permanent in the world.

CHAPTER THIRTEEN

EDUCATION WITHOUT STRENGTH: A ONE-WING BIRD

Growing up as a child, I was made to believe, by my community and family members, that education and spirituality are supreme. Though I never believed in formal education and never went to school, I read as much as possible, be it history, religion, spirituality, philosophy, literature, or astrology. I looked upon intelligence as the only goal for every human being in life, until I found a lot from my own community meek, who, for hundreds of years, merely used education as a tool to earn their stripes. Thus, I was confronted with an age-old question, isn't intelligence without strength like a bird with one of its wings afflicted? The bird, of course, can't fly long, and then, we are reminded of the history of Tibet and India as well, with all their truth and wisdom, having been trampled by the muddy feet of imperialism and colonialism.

Distorted and misconstrued though it may sound, no intelligence can survive without strength, be it through peace, through diplomacy, or through violence. It remains an undiluted fact that almost all the religions in the world grew through the warrior class, and barely through direct dissemination or teaching. Whereas the example of Buddhism and Hinduism is one of peaceful dissemination, the trails of the religions of the Arab world and the West turn out to be different, but the commonality is that all these religions flourished well under the tutelage of rulers themselves. Ostensibly, we can't deny the role of different religions in producing different rulers of different characters either—the factors behind the distinction between Indian rulers like Prithviraj Chauhan and rulers like Bakhtiyar Khalji.

Suppose a brutally injured young man hiding himself behind bushes catches the attention of a sannyasin in a dense forest and the latter is asked by a group of armed men if he has seen anyone passing by. The sannyasin's dharma is to stand by Satya (truth), but in this pursuit, he may end up being a cause of Ahimsa (violence) when his dharma is also to be free from violence. A great dilemma, thus, for the freaks of metaphysics, should the sannyasin stand by truth in view of his dharma and be a cause of violence, or should he speak untruth, thus deviating from his dharma, and avoid violence? How important is truth where peace, and the natural order of Nature, is challenged by it?

In many instances, we may also be compelled to accept the unquestioned importance of violence. Suppose one individual gets killed by another in the name of non-violence, the former believing that non-violence is supreme. It is conspicuous that the killing is but violence itself to a third individual observing all. Alternatively, suppose a king who is the only reason behind peace in his state gets killed by a group of men in the name of non-violence. His killing undoubtedly may lead to extreme chaos in an otherwise peaceful state, and so the only solution may be one of being violent to assassins before any assassination.

Since we have already been programmed to regard dharma in a certain way, conditioned to believe it to be either truth or non-violence, we need to reassess all the cacophonies of different political and non-political streams of thought. Unfortunately, amid the hue and cry of the 21st century and our burning desire to be listened to and looked at, we end up being liberals, rightists, or leftists without any scientific inquiry. Thus, we are guided like the sheep of Himachal Pradesh, comfortable and alluring yet unable to walk independently.

CHAPTER FOURTEEN

ARE WE LIVING WHOLISTICALLY?

Working as a professional astrologist for over a decade now, I have connected to clients from all spheres of life. Businessmen, sportsmen, saints, offenders, addicts, the depressed, the ambitious, the spiritually serious, the poor, the rich, the diseased, and the healthy, all of them suffered from sorrow in one way or another, and that implied that anything outside in the world is incapable of obliterating our sorrow. Moreover, their lives are limited by their own professional, familial, social and psychological conditioning. A lawyer tends to think that the whole world is only about courts, lawyers, and judges; a priest tends to think that there is no world beyond his rituals, temple, scriptures, and dogmas; and a doctor ends up limiting their life to only their hospital and medicines.

Our brains start functioning like computers programmed by certain experts to perform certain actions, so that any actions that our brains are not programmed for become impossible for us. This is where we witness we are limited in all ways, and because we are limited, we end up limiting others. Those appearing to be free from limitation created by the social, religious, educational, ideological, political, and psychological orders start to seem to be great threats to our own existence. For instance, if one is a staunch atheist, there comes about a subconscious repel in one's life from a theist, because the latter begin to weaken the very psychological structure, or what we call the psychological self, of the former.

Not many of us may have looked into what we after all call the 'Self'. Suppose we have Mr. A with a lot of land, property, wealth, degrees, respect, and supporters; what is the actual self of Mr A? Of course, the biology and physiology of Mr. A, but apart from these, the psychological self as well. The psychological self is premised upon the question, what does Mr. A identify himself to? His bank balance, property, lands, supporters, education, degrees, and so on and so forth. The greater or stronger the identifications in both quantity and quality, the greater the value and existence of Mr. A. However, we can now ask another question, what is Mr. A if all the above identifications are taken away, like his supporter, wealth and the rest? Clearly, psychologically, Mr. A then is nothing—absolutely nothing.

The self therefore has a tendency to enlarge itself by consuming more and more identifications. The more it identifies, the more satisfied it feels and thus the more existent. Surprisingly, the self itself is a bundle of identifications, and the end of identifications implies the end of the self, and the self is always afraid of the end, so we see anything about one in an opposition to the ideology or belief of another is a matter of discomfort to the latter. Thus, the long-persistent clashes between the Catholics and the Protestants, the Shias and the Sunnis, the Hinayana and the Mahayana, and a lot more.

The self according to its own identifications finds itself more comfortable in groups with similar orientations. For instance, a leftist is going to feel more empowered and stable in a group of other staunch leftists, and quite uncomfortable by rightists. So even the unconscious choices as to the movements of the psychological and physical self is ascertained only by the deepest identifications.

I am reminded of a friend who came up to me a month ago asking me for advice over a new job opportunity offering him twice the then salary. I got him two options to either join the company with the offer but with no work-life balance or wait for ten months until the company he worked at offered him a robust increment. He chose the first option—that of accepting the latest offer. A month after his joining, he came up to me and burst into tears, badmouthing his boss, calling his life ruined, and depressed. All I had to say to him, "My friend, you chose that option. You chose the situation you are in right now."

Either consciously or unconsciously, knowingly or unknowingly, we choose our sorrow or happiness; we are the sole reason behind all our sorrow or happiness in the world. We alone choose the events, situations and people of our lives, and it is thus most likely that what we are facing right now was already chosen by us years, months, days, or minutes ago. Mysterious indeed are the ways of the self, then. It takes the credit for all that is pleasant around it and blames everything and everybody around for all that is unpleasant. It keeps moving between two extremes like the pendulum, the mid-location being that of freedom, tranquillity, and timelessness.

The very movements of the self are a deterrent to living wholistically. A doctor may fail to live a non-doctor way;

a lawyer may fail to live a non-lawyer way; and a religious individual may fail to live all ways that are in opposition to his dogmas and scriptures. This is greatest for survival and evolution, but not for being one with life completely.

CHAPTER FIFTEEN

WHAT IS BEYOND DEATH?

Most of the times, we fail to observe anything wholistically, and there appears therefore a distortion in our own observation owing to different factors as a result of our past. Due to these distortions, we fail to be one with reality and thus life itself.

There was a point of time when Indian society was never reluctant to divulge the complexities and simplicity of death and sexuality, but over several decades, there arose numerous saints with little awareness who isolated the men and women of this society from the day-to-day conducts observed upon death and from the understanding of sexuality within each and every organism on the planet. Isolation implies lack of oneness, which in turn, implies lack of understanding. This is how most men and women in our society lost touch with the spiritual essence of the land.

If death happens during our lifetime, it must be part of life itself, and so must birth. Both death and birth must be part of life, just like the subsiding and rising of waves in a sea. The sea goes on, but the waves go on disappearing and appearing in different forms and shapes. The whole world similarly may be looked upon as a sea, with no separation anywhere, so the planets in the solar system exist within us and we exist within those planets. Without sunlight, there could be no photosynthesis, without photosynthesis, there could be no growth of food to eat, and without food, survival is out of the question. Through that sunlight, the Sun exists within us, and in the same way, the whole world is one, so the Hindus proclaim, *"Yatt Pinde Tatt Brahmaande,"* whereas the Sikhs proclaim, *"Ek Omkar,"* and Jesus proclaimed, *"My father and I are one."*

If there is impermanence all around, that is, if there is change every second, every second everything changing, where is death? That is, when we use the word 'death', we imply something permanent and static coming to an end, but if there is nothing static and permanent, where is death or where is that which dies? Could it be that death exists only within the mind, and not outside?

Of course, there is biological death, since an organism dies, but this also is a biological fact that there is constant replenishment within each and every organism on this planet through the cells and tissues it contains, and thus, there is no biological permanence either. Therefore, it seems that the picture of something being permanent and static is only our incapability to be one with the constant change all around in the world. It is like a mirage or dream, far from any reality in existence.

I am not the same individual today while writing this chapter as I was while writing the first or even the previous chapter. Some have truly said, "You cannot cross the same river twice."

Nothing is created in this world, and nothing can be destroyed; all we have is constant transformation. Therefore, we always invoke the word 'Shaanti!' three times in Hindu culture: Shaanti! Shaanti! Shaanti! No creation or destruction in the past, the present, or the future. This also implies that life goes on, containing its lap both death and birth, coming from eternity going to eternity. We are eternal, and the Upanishad beautifully proclaims, "Satyam Gyaanam Anantam Brahma."

CHAPTER SIXTEEN

THE RELATION BETWEEN THE CONSCIOUS AND THE UNCONSCIOUS

I recall a conversation I had a couple of months ago with an Indian advocate unfortunately suffering from acute kidney complications in her late thirties. Unmarried and somewhat financially unsettled, she was confused about the future and thought I could help her through my expertise of Astrology. I did not deny either and had a look at her chart to only find out that life for her was going to be worse soon, but I could not reveal my reading honestly to her, for instead of helping her, it would have destroyed whatever happy moments of her life she was left with. I am not sure if most astrologers around do the same with this understanding of psychology, especially when it is about something that cannot at all be changed.

As she progressed in the conversation with me, she professed that most discoveries in the world have already been made and that there is nothing much left to find out and inquire into. This was a typical mentality that every Indian at the beginning of the 21st century carries, and this has become a deterrent to their curiosity and thirst for wisdom. When we believe that we have already reached, there is no point of further moving anywhere, the consequence being stagnancy and lack of creativity.

Indians through some decades now have considered education as only a tool to fill their stomach, and a tool is meant to be thrown away or kept aside as soon as its utility is over; this is precisely what is going on in India and is likely to prevail unless all stomachs are filled and the country has enough for everybody. Certainly, rarely have we seen creativity and curiosity prevail unless the stomach is full.

Since for several generations education has been used merely as a tool for survival for most of us, we have been programmed to stick and cling to the old, without even realizing that there is no possibility for anything new so long as we do not free ourselves from the old.

Our educational system across the globe has trained us to be competitive, and to be competitive means to conform or imitate, and imitation and conformation mean the repetition or replication of the old, therefore missing out on the opportunities to be creative and discover anything new.

The known, that is, all that we have known so far, must be the old, and its constant pursuance implies distance from the unknown, that is, all that we have not known so far. Not only that, thought, as response from memory, being the sum total of all our experiences, always works in the realm of the known. Thought has very little room for creativity, and we thus say that creativity is born only beyond the horizon of the known, the old, and thoughts.

Psychologists today accept that ninety-five percent of our consciousness is unconscious and only five percent is conscious. They mean to point out that ninety five percent of our experiences since the beginning of our existence are so far unavailable to us in the form of memory. For instance, if I am greedy of five lakh rupees, someone else may be greedy of ten lakh rupees, but greed is common to both of us. If greed here is part of our collective consciousness, greed of either five lakh rupees or ten lakh rupees is part of individual consciousness. The waves may appear different on the surface of the ocean must be the same deep down in the ocean.

If I am greedy, fearful, jealous, angry, insecure, aggressive, lusty, lonely, possessive, so are other, and so is the whole world. We share the majority of our consciousness and call it collective consciousness, out of which plausibly appears individual consciousness.

The Naasadiya Sukta of the Rigveda proclaims, "Where is this world coming from? Where is it going? Perhaps he who is sitting in the highest heaven knows, or perhaps even he does not, since he, too, came into existence only after the Creation." The world existed for billions of years before the advent of human beings, and it will go on wondrously well even after human beings completely fade away from the face of the earth, but through millions of years of our evolution, we have had imprints of so many experiences our species went through, in different forms like Orangutans, Homo Neanderthals, Denisovans, four-legged species, and numerous simpler life forms. The memories of our journey for millions of years to this day must be there in our unconscious, because all those experiences are the sole reason behind what we are today: Homo sapience. We carry within us the whole history of our existence, though all we have access to so far is the memories of only a couple of decades.

It is undeniable that a lot that happened even during the two world wars, eventually resulting in the Industrial Revolution, has shaped even Indians, despite the fact that Indians had no active role whatsoever in the wars. The ways we dress, speak, write, and live are the results of the psychological evolution of the past itself. We carry the effects of the traumas of the two world wars in our collective consciousness so far.

Science today accepts that all that humans can observe is only five percent of all that exists around, that only a miniscule portion of reality is accessible to humans. This is a testament to the fact that there is a lot more to discover and be curious about. In fact, the very beginning of a spiritual journey must be curiosity itself. However, we ask ourselves, are our students and we all as curious as we were in our early teenage and before?

As we grow up, our minds are filled with the old—old notions, prejudices, norms, ideologies, and a lot more information necessary for the survival—but it is a fact that survival is not life and does not mean being one with life itself. Ostensibly, we become what we accumulate, both physiologically and psychologically, and this is where there comes about a gap between the old that we are and the new that life is every second before is. The old, for its own protection and survival, starts resisting the new and goes on losing curiosity. This is the reason why most of those from Bihar and Uttar Pradesh are barely into creative pursuits, since the struggle for survival and the need for protection are stronger there, and this prevails in most of India. An inkling for the same could also be there with a simple question, "How many Indians have read more than ten books in the last twelve months?"

CHAPTER SEVENTEEN

EVOLUTION OF HOMO SAPIENCE

When vigorous alpha males hunted for their expecting alpha females thousands of years ago, they must have thought themselves the smartest with the enceinte thinking themselves the luckiest. Undeniable may be the proposition that there must have been continual struggles for superiority, among both males and females. The best among the masculine must have been those with the strongest bodies for hunting and protecting their mates, and the best among the feminine must have been those with the largest breasts indicative of a great capability to be nurturing mothers. To this day, thus, men's obsession with the breasts of women, and women's obsession with security, be it financial, physical, psychological, or sexual.

With no other parameters for superiority, the bodies must have been the greatest determinant, and it was all certainly more than enough for stability and safety and livelihood. However, the course of evolution seems to have changed, like the narrow alleys of the ancient city of Benares, right after the discovery of agricultural revolution. The revolution evoked permanent settlement, and thus our ancestors were blessed with an unexpected providential up-gradation from being hunter-gatherers to being farmers. It of course marked the beginning of a family-culture, and amid it all, the struggle for superiority took altogether different shape. Men with larger agricultural stocks, and not only with strong physiques, came into the picture. The most evolved among them endeavored to discover a science for better production, more precise weather reports, and suitable time periods for various activities like reaping, sowing, and conceiving. This, to me, appears to be the very womb of Vedic Astrology, in India, as well — a wonderful form of apparent astronomy.

The agricultural revolution seems to have brought stability and developed linguistic consciousness, in our ancestors, capable of speaking, reading, and writing even partial languages like signs, symbols, and digits now. Those obsessed with sharpest tools for hunting could be found with the subtle art of painting, speaking, symbolism, and writing — thus an ostensible softness in their nature. They now were a lot more than merely their bodies and thus pure instinct, affected significantly by the birth of their intellect. Here, once again, as we see, the parameters for superiority increase with the addition of linguistic capabilities, observational skills, and intellect.

All the way to globalization and the technological, scientific and industrial revolutions after the agricultural and linguistic revolutions, we apparently seem to have come a long way, but the question is, are we completely free from all our instinctive endeavors of the primitive time? Have women given up the subtlety of seeking security, and have men put an end to the grossness of flaunting their superiority?

The ways of men even today appear to be gross and noisy, and those of women, subtle and silent. It goes without saying that there is conspicuous cunningness and cleverness in both sexes, since the ways of jungles must now continue to exist more silently and therefore inwardly. But it is irrefutable that that which is subtle and silent is always more dangerous, more damaging, and less understandable. Not only that, the evolutionary course has ensured that women must act out of their fast-changing emotionality and men out of their steadfast, rigid logic, which makes it more difficult for a man to tackle a woman. The very nature of a woman's being turns dynamic, her calling a man unjust in the morning and declaring him the best in the world on the very same evening. This puts her in a great dilemma: that of being indecisive. The volatile, capricious nature of a woman thus here finds balance, security, and stability in the rigidness of a man.

Despite the fact that the watery emotionality of women may find stability by the dry logic of men, women instinctively have known numerous ways to keep men under control and desirably continual checks. Even with their dependence for thousands of years on men, they made sure they had control over resources, so to this day, we see its repercussions in women being the greatest enemies of women in families and workplaces. We wonder if it is a lot more than a mere petty struggle for greater control over resources.

Had the fair sex not been the very source of procreation, they would perhaps been obliterated by the masculine a long time ago, like the likely extinction of Neanderthals at the blood-drenched hands of Homo Sapiens. Of course, they have had their own stories of struggles on this course of evolution, and have therefore developed their own subtle and perhaps more cunning ways to be safer and more secure. Gone is the time when cows were most attracted to bulls that bugled the loudest.

CHAPTER EIGHTEEN

THE ROLE OF EVOLUTION IN SPIRITUALITY

Many of us even today fail to realize that we were not millions of years ago what we are today—that we did not walk on two legs, did not have such short teeth, did not cultivate, and did not wear t-shirts and chinos. A majority of us so far tend to believe that the world began this way and must end the same way as well. There was a point of time when organized religions, especially in the West, were made insecure about their own notions and beliefs by the theory of evolution and evolutionary scientists. They long tried to resist the pursuance of the theory of evolution at schools there, until recently it became part of their curricula.

There was a time when some believed that the world began with humans and must end with humans or their gods themselves, and the notion prevailed within most minds in the West and laymen in the Indian subcontinent, but the Theory of Evolution proves now that the Universe existed for aeons before the advent of humans and that it will go on wondrously well even after humans completely fade away. The Theory of Evolution proves humans to be mere spectators or actors in the play of life, and not the director, and since the world existed for an infinite time before their arrival, to trace the beginning of life is almost out of the question. Any attempt to answer the question as to who created the universe must be a product of the conditioning of the human mind. For Americans, the creator may have white skin, for the Chinese, slant eyes, and for the Indians, brown skin.

Change seems to be unchangeable, unstoppable, invincible, but there are still millions of us attempting round the clock at being the fiercest antagonists of the natural order. Not only do we find comfort and insecurity in culturism and traditionalism — especially if we are old-aged — but also we love to impose our idiosyncrasies as to the atmosphere we are brought up in. We carry badges of the communities, states, and religions we belong to, never inquiring into the very psychological drive behind our pomp.

It's clear that a mind encumbered by a particular culture and tradition is not only uncreative and unscientific, to an extent, but also dead, for everything alive affords change and modification. The culturally fanatic mind says that there should be no changes at all, and that there is no change either. Thus, it turns out to be a deterrent to creativity and discovery, unaware of the fact that truth, or whatever is existential, is independent of all authorities, be they organized religions, gurus, scriptures, or states. Moreover, such a mind, programmed by society, is mechanical and repetitive as well, bringing about all the flawed social institutions around us.

This also remains a reality that most organized religions across the globe have tried their best to touch the essence of the source of all that there is, thus calling the source Eternity, Omnipresence, or Omnipotence. The Hindus have looked inwards and found that which is beyond the impermanence of the body and the mind—the witness of all the impermanence in the world. It has been clear to Hindus that life is far beyond the activities of the mind and the body, and to go beyond the limitations of the mind and the body, they must observe both the body and the mind.

The evolved Hindus in their meditation realized a general principle that we are free from whatever is completely, wholistically observed by us. Suppose you look at this book currently reading it, you are not this book and can handle it as a result of your freedom, putting it anywhere and flipping its pages. In the same way, when we merely observe our breath, body, bodily sensations, thoughts, and emotions, we start getting free from them, instead of being glued to them all and swayed or controlled by them as if were on auto-mode as per the programming of consciousness.

If you have to fight an individual with a sword, you must have him stand in front of you. To fight, you need to cling to the object you are fighting against. In the same way, when we fight, we end up clinging to our mind and body, never getting free. Meditation means the end of all fights, with the general principle that we are free and distant from all that we observe wholistically.

What distinguishes us from our ancestors millions of years ago is our inherent capability now to think. Perhaps we can now store far more information than our ancestors can and memory span is far longer. This is evident in other organisms like cats and dogs which have perhaps far shorter memory spans than humans today. This long memory span was a blessing to us to store more and more information and use it for our survival more efficiently. It was all part of our evolution.

However, we must understand that life went on even before the development of our intellect and must have its source in what is far beyond intellect as well. To go beyond our intellect, we must be aware of it, that is, we must observe it wholistically, instead of being entangled in its subconscious and unconscious patterns. To be simple and effortless, therefore, becomes indispensable and any effort to be free must be another movement of our own conditioning in lieu of observing the mind and getting free from it.

We have come a long way on the scale of evolution—from being purely instinctive to being intellectual—and it is now high time that we should evolve further going beyond intellect as well.

CHAPTER NINETEEN

THE MANEUVERS OF ELITISM — A TRAIL OF PROPAGANDAS

It's evolutionary that in every region, out of social mobility, there spring up a few economically, socially, and psychologically dominant people called elites. These elites come together and then bring about a social structure known as a culture, by calling all their rituals, practices, and lifestyles refined and therefore the most evolved. As time passes by, with their culture as a tool, they start identifying and isolating numerous groups of other people who they think belong in different societies.

The elites seek to control and oppress every foreign group, treating it as an outcaste. As they are well aware that their dominance is premised upon the social order created by them, they soon begin to propagandize in the name of culturism and traditionalism. No stones are left unturned to make sure that only they have the right to their rituals and practices; thus, there come about two conspicuous layers of a particular society—the oppressors and the oppressed.

The division between the oppressors and the oppressed goes on, educationally, economically, and socially, the former blatantly, and sometimes aggressively, maintaining that their social status is monolithic. Amidst all this, out of self-caused blindness, the elites also go on denying that they themselves were once purely cultureless, that the culture they ask others to uphold with ineffably great reverence was but created by them for their own security and power.

The Varna System, having prevailed in the Indian Subcontinent for more than 1400 years, the casteism deeply ingrained in our minds today, and the racism of the West, are all indicative of the same division out of the intellectual evolution of human beings. Human beings, too, like apes and orangutans — their ancestors — have long believed in political congregations, and the desire for power sought by alpha males.

Once hunter-gatherers, moving on to accidentally discovering fire, Homo sapiens began their political career with the idea of agriculture, where they would need to have semi-permanent settlements and thus manpower for security. Who knew then that the same group of animals would get so evolved one day that they would end up leaving a trail of footprints on the moon and calling themselves the creator of the Universe? Is it also possible that, just like humans, if cows had got so evolved accidentally, she would also be compelled to think today that the creator of the universe must have had four legs and two horns?

Not denying that the Varna System may have been useful in various contexts in the past, a simple apparition is that it was used for oppression and ostracization as well. At the same time, there have been many evidences as to atrocities having been perpetrated for years in the West in the name of racial superiority.

Homo sapiens may still not be as evolved as they think they are. Moreover, the Universe existed for billions of years before the advents of humans and their religions and their gods, and it will go on wonderfully well without them as well, sheltering thousands of other animals, like humans, and their gods in the future.

CHAPTER TWENTY

HUMAN INTELLECT AS ARTIFICIAL INTELLIGENCE TAKES OVER

We have indeed come a long way, from making tools of stones to creating Artificial intelligence soon to be capable enough to replace humans at most workplaces. We may look back on the way horses were replaced by motor vehicles during the industrial revolution in the West, and humans may be baffled by the time they realize that almost all activities performed by them, no matter whether these are intellectual, artistic, manual, or military, are going to be taken over by Artificial Intelligence soon. We are perhaps not sure whether we are going to write a decade later the way I have written this book today, and that time in the future is going to challenge us with the futility of human intellect.

Why would be human intellect preferred to Artificial Intelligence, when most activities can be performed by the latter in far more efficient way. After all, all that humans need is efficiency and productivity, and since machines and algorithms cannot have mood swings, cannot fall sick, and may last far longer than humans, they are likely to be preferred in almost all human pursuits.

A single click of a button would be enough to hack the cybersecurity of the defence system of a whole country, and algorithms inscrutable to financial experts and bankers would reject loan-applications leaving the applicants perplexed. Power may then not be as distributed as it is today. Trade unions, for instance, can go against the working conditions and yield great power against any injustice in the trade relations, but when most vehicles are by a handful through Artificial Intelligence, the capability to control and make changes would be in fewer hands.

Humans are soon going to ask, what is the difference between organic algorithms (human consciousness) and inorganic algorithms (Artificial Intelligence) at the peak of the latter's evolution, especially all that the world needs is more efficiency and productivity. There looms a time that may render humans futile and open to accepting the fact that they need to move beyond the realm of intellect. It may of course pave the way to new jobs and new human pursuits.

Apart from the above, there is likely to be a great tussle between Artificial Intelligence and humans when the former reaches its utmost state of evolution, where it can strike off the latter from the face of the earth completely. Let us talk about a recent example of how Artificial Intelligence has been found out to promote on social media only those posts that induce more and more greed, fear, aggression, and fanaticism, since viewers are more likely to watch only such content also recommended to them on and on.

The other question is, what are humans going to do in the state of their futility as Artificial Intelligence takes over? Are they going to be confined to drugs and entertainment as an escape from their sorrow and the feeling of uselesness?

CHAPTER TWENTY-ONE

YOU ARE THE WORLD

About 2100 years ago, when Jews sat at the temple of Jerusalem, they said, and were rather sure, that the sun rose for the earth every day because they read the Talmud. Tens of other organized religions sprang up—both in Asia and in Europe—after the holy edifices of Judea were shattered into pieces by the Roman Empire, some of them having had the same tone as the Jews had. However, the flux of time spared little fanaticism of the religions and made it conspicuous that truth, non-violence, compassion, and love are all independent of all authorities.

No language, culture, tradition, and nation can have a monopoly on truth. The sun rising every day, the birds chirping over our heads, the clouds hovering in the vastness of the sky, and the trees dancing to the soporific breeze have nothing whatsoever to do with human intellect. At the same time, it's the fecundity of human intellect to say that Dharma can be preserved by it, whereas humans themselves, along with other creatures, are the result of thousands of years of evolution. It's but the cosmic intelligence, and not humans as the centre of the universe, behind the sustenance of all that there is.

Like a wave being a whole ocean, an individual is psychologically the whole world as well. All of us share the same content of consciousness, that is, we all carry within us envy, fear, greed, loneliness, and insecurity, which implies we are all the same, with different bodies and different colours. Thus, the wars, riots, and chaos outside are but the outward forms of the content of our own consciousness.

The very essence of a society is its culture and tradition, and its structure is conspicuously premised upon the content of human consciousness. Human consciousness, with greed, fear, envy, jealousy, loneliness and possessiveness as its content, has evolved through thousands of years and brought about all the societal norms, structures and institutions in the outside world. Therefore, the world outside can also be compared to the webs of a spider.

As the mind has created all our cultures and traditions, out of its inward poverty and chaos, it makes sure that nothing changes in society. This way, it successfully finds its comfort, security, and escape from its chaos. However, it loses touch with all that is natural, for it remains extremely absorbed in what has been created by it. Then, it is always out of touch with all that has not been created by it—the sun, the moon, the clouds, the trees dancing to a soporific breeze in its garden.

As is clear now, an individual who is deeply absorbed in their culture and tradition must be out of touch with everything natural. This is startling in view of the fact that what has been created by the mind—its culture and tradition—is not even a speck of dust before all that has not been created by it—before all that is natural. Such an individual, therefore, is a deterrent to creativity and scientific discovery, when they are merely mechanical, repetitive, or robotic. Their being robotic is what we call conditioning or programming.

An individual encumbered with culture and tradition is dead while being dangerous for everything alive, as they will seek to exploit everything natural as per their convenience or inward chaos or poverty. At the same time, all this implies that they will stand against all the forces that lead to natural changes out of evolution. Standing against the force of intellectual evolution, they will fiercely, blatantly uphold and justify their religious orders put together by them in the name of divinity—the creator of the universe, who they think must be a perfect human being.

Interestingly, human beings think that the creator of the universe must be another human being when they themselves arrived merely around 5 million years ago in the universe, which has had a history of at least 13 billion years. Thousands of species—like those of dinosaurs, of course— got sheltered by the earth before the arrival of Homo sapiens, but Homo sapiens think that they are the creator or centre of the universe. Why not some other creature or species which had been existential long before the advent of human beings?

Had cows got accidentally evolved as humans did, they would confidently have said that the creator of the universe must be white with a magical tail and golden horns. They would also be worshipping their fancy gods out of their greed and fear, just as human beings do.

As is obvious, Homo sapiens are bound to deny evolution as well, which they are often seen doing in their religious world. In fact, the whole theory of evolution is a threat to the religious and cultural propagandas brought about by human consciousness out of its poverty. Human beings would never like to hear that they are as ordinary as any other animal on the earth, be it an ant or an orangutan.

CHAPTER TWENTY-TWO

INNOCENCE LOST

If we are looted twice by strangers in the dead of night, we must be aggressive the third time a stranger knocks at our door even at dawn. The aggression within is but the very fear that we may be looted again, thus leading us to build numerous tall walls for isolation.

Since we have all been looted several times, most of us have already built our walls—those of cunningness, fear, jealousy, callousness, anger, frustration, overambition, possessiveness, and insecurity. We are triggered merely at the sight of strangers passing through our alleys, let alone them stopping by for resting under the scorching sun.

The innocence that most of us have lost was perhaps a priceless gift of Mother Nature, and the walls we have built have already separated us from the very source of life. I wonder, then, at times, if we are alive machines or dead humans round the clock waiting for the darkness of night to prove to our neighbours the strength of our walls.

According to Buddhist historical accounts, when Angulimaal, a murderer who chopped off fingers, approached Gautama the Buddha to kill him, the latter looked into his eyes and iterated that he had suffered a lot. Angulimaal was shunned by the words of Gautama, and found himself unable to deny any of them. He, who until then believed in humans only being crude and cruel, for the first time had come across someone who could look into the darkest corners of his heart. Not only was it the realization that he had hurt and killed hundreds of humans out of his hurt but it also led him to complete enlightenment. He is mentioned to have been called *ahimsak* after his renunciation as well.

Humankind today seems to have a lot of Angulimaals, doesn't it? The etymology of the word "innocence" is described as "a mind incapable of being hurt", as a mind with no trace of any sort of hurt can never hurt other minds. One can give others only that which one has, so thus says the poet eternally closest to my heart, "Those who give you a serpent when you ask for a fish, may have nothing but serpents to give. It is then generosity on their part."

I wonder how many of you not in your twenties have come across those in their twenties with strong tendencies to thug. I say, it was never so prominent in any generation for several reasons. We perhaps never had youths so melancholic either, until the world changed overnight after the advent of technology and globalization. Though great that there is more self-awareness today, evolution has brought us to a point where the toxicity inherited by today's youth from their immediate ancestors is more pivotal in society than ever.

This also seems to be an era, led by the youth, dedicated to the strongest forms of escapism, or pleasure, be it sex, addiction, casual relationships, overambition or workplace politics. The more frustrated a youth is, the greater their desire to escape from their frustration. Then, it is merely a daydream to expect the youth to be in love with their art, music, or literature.

Our escapism is merely a race to a destination that exists nowhere in reality, our search for security leads to greater insecurity, and our ambition to be at the top brings us down to numerous abysses. Our happiness that we think lies in goals and people outside is as large a mirage as one often to a thirsty recluse in a secluded desert under a scorching sun. The whole world that appears to be dead to the old seems to be a dream to the youth, and my heart says that neither of the approaches has any life.

We hold on to what we think is our happiness and expect nothing to change, when the existence of the universe is premised only upon change every second. This becomes our best way to add to the sorrow already within us. Objects and people outside keep slipping off and our desire to turn the changeable into the unchangeable becomes stronger and stronger, until we come across a providential crossroad in light in the lore of evolution. Certainly, a flower blossoms only in the lap of Mother Nature and its petals cannot be forcibly opened even by the gentlest hands, otherwise its destiny turns out to be that of the face of one dead inwardly with a nine-to-five job for a reason even one's deepest self is unaware of.

I once came across a young lady insecure about herself in her married life, and I was told by her that the best she could do to keep the interest of her partner in her alive was to join the best gym around 10 kilometers away from her home. She added that she was not happy about her appearance; and she was sure that she did not get enough attention for the same reason. Whereas her solution, that of joining the gym, sounds logical to most of us, I feel that the real problem was within her, that of insecurity. Undeniably, her partner's dissatisfaction, on the other hand, was another great problem poisonous to the very wholesomeness of his life. I sounded there rather old-fashioned and boring talking about meditation and being free from insecurity, jealousy, fear, possessiveness, anger and eventually the mind itself.

While Diarrhoea in the body most of the times plays a crucial role in clearing the bacteria found in the intestines, Mental Diarrhoea becomes more and more poisonous with time, deterring us from even living life. It never lets us realize that all our endeavours in the world have only one goal, that of being more and more joyous, and one with life. In order to have more joy, in our somnambulism, we end up losing all our joy, eventually forgetting why we start a voyage.

The more we run after respect and companionship, the more we run away from disrespect and abandonment, when all the four are impermanent and exist merely for a while. Our running away is also our sorrow, our not liking others' words and acts labelled by our minds as disrespect and abandonment respectively. Therefore, our desire to have happiness, positivity, stability, respect and companionship exists only so long as there is, in the eyes of our mind, sorrow, negativity, instability, disrespect and abandonment. Our desire to have happiness is merely an escape from our sorrow, instead of the eradication of sorrow. There is no happiness anywhere in the world, but the absence of sorrow is joy itself.

CHAPTER TWENTY-THREE

WILLINGNESS TO GIVE UP

Amrapali is often referred to as the most beautiful woman to have lived in the history of India. According to Buddhist historical accounts, she was born in Vaishali, the capital city of the Republic of Licchavi, in around 500 BC. It is said she grew up to be a woman of ineffable charm and grace, and was blessed with exceptional artistic abilities.

She had been declared a Nagarvadhu, or the bride of a city, of Vaishali, and numerous kings and princes from distant lands died to be by her. Though merely another courtesan, a Nagarvadhu in that time was treated like a goddess, but as per the traditions, she could not commit herself to one single man at all.

We also get to learn that when Bimbisara, the King of Magadha, attacked Licchavi, his hostile neighbour, he took refuge in Amrapali's mansion. However, having already fallen in love with Amrapali, upon her request, he receded eventually. The king later on was killed by his son, Ajatashatru, the latter falling in love with Amrapali and attacking the city once again.

There are some historical accounts that confirm the presence of Amrapali at the wedding of Gautama the Buddha, and it is said that she was then mesmerized by the purity of his character and love for his wife, Yashodhara. Though she had all that even numerous kings merely dreamt of in the world, she for the first time in her life had felt that she was never loved, that she was merely a delight for the eyes, and not for the hearts, of her attendees.

Amrapali's unmatched beauty had turned out to be a curse in many ways, and she had realized that it was only her body that allured the world around. Therefore, she, years later, started following Gautama the Buddha's teachings and renounced in order to be an arahant eventually. It was freedom from her insecurity about losing her beauty and thus the attention and respect she received.

Ostensibly, anything looked upon as an object to fulfil the needs of the human mind must be a mere tool which is often thrown off when it is not required. There is so much to learn for today's generation from the anecdote from Amrapali's life, for most of us of late are deeply identified with our bodies as well. We think that having great physicality and thus alluring figures is the best way to sell and buy relationships, without even realizing that such relationships must be premised only upon superficiality.

Where we are used to being tools for satisfaction, either physical or psychological, there is no possibility of love at all. Love certainly is not commerce.

CHAPTER TWENTY-FOUR

LOVE TO THE FULLEST

I have never been a great believer in the institution of marriage, nor have I ever considered it a significant or rather inevitable part of life. Though marriage has for thousands of years served as a great tool for a robust social order, premised upon the essence of regional culture, tradition and religion, the history of evolution has witnessed women being merely their husbands' properties pledged by their fathers. Certainly, the history of marriage is not as pure as marriage itself is deemed today.

As Homo sapiens yearned for permanent settlements in view of their agrarian pursuits, they felt the need for law and order. Out of this need were drawing in hundreds of revered tangible and intangible social and religious institutions of today whose stability depended only upon our respect for them. Therefore, it was paramount for humankind to consider the origins of the institutions divine.

Today, I see, the whole social order brought about by the needs of human consciousness is weakening. We are now more and more inclined to independence — both psychological and social — and, with duality being ubiquitous, we are going to face both the negative and the positive. We are perhaps never going to be back to the time when a brother-in-law considered the wife of his brother his mother in Indian culture. It was a time when fidelity was still put on a pedestal by the majority, and sexual desperation, out of inward gloom, was not as strong as it is today. Eventually, then, I think, we are all making for a society with more and more nuclear families.

Long considered as an essential part of *Dharma* in a culture like that of India, marriage has plausibly played a great role in the lives of individuals. India, that is, Bharat, is where the *Creator* has been realized to be *Ardhnarishwar,* which means half a man and half a woman, or the union of a man and a woman. Marriage here has been looked upon as a pure path to the Ultimate Freedom, that of a wave being the whole ocean, that of the individual self merging with the *Ultimate Self*. It beautifully divulges how evolution, and Existence itself, is out of the question if the feminine and the masculine do not walk hand in hand.

I see tens of married couples around me perplexed, gloomy and depressed. Not only are they hesitant to openly talk about their conjugal lives but they also unknowingly move towards infidelity out of immense dissatisfaction. It is saddening to see them burying their heads into their pillows in the dead of night, as if the blind were standing in the middle of a crossroad. In a time like, thus, my heart asks a question to you all. What is the future of the institution of marriage?

Love, to most of us, is like a grand North Indian Thali, pompously serving rasagulla, raita, pickles, and at times a couple of pieces of meat as well. How delicious! However, we can eat only if our stomach is empty, that is, when there is a physiological need, and not when our stomach is full. Emptiness is a determinant, then, isn't?

We say that love is comfort and hope when we fail to see that the very reason behind clinging to comfort is discomfort. Running away from darkness, we run after light; running away from disrespect, we run after respect; and running away from disaffection and abandonment, we run after affection and validation. On the other hand, running away implies sorrow and immense suffering, so we suffer day in, day out in a world rooted in duality-that of light and darkness, men and women, and heat and cold. Plausibly, the existence of the Universe is out of the question without this duality as well.

Now, it is an elementary question: Is love attachment? Attachment means the want of some kind of continuity-the desire for the continuity of what we like. For instance, one has had a pathetic childhood, full of disaffection, one is sitting with one's girlfriend or boyfriend under a shaggy tree on a lovely day, and this is something one likes immensely as one has already developed a tendency to run away from disaffection. Unfortunately, the companion passes away the following day and there comes an end to their affection as well. What follows here is but immense suffering as one has already got attached, which gets manifested as ineffable, inexplicable loneliness.

At the same time, when one is lonely, one steps out and clings to and thus depends upon what one likes, running away from loneliness. This dependence results in attachment, and attachment brings about the fear of losing what one is dependent upon, and the fear leads to possessiveness, insecurity, jealousy, and various other kinds of neurotic chaos which lead to further loneliness. Moreover, we should be clear about the fact that attachment always results in fear - the fear of losing what we are attached to. The very nature of attachment is thus, as there is impermanence all around.

Certainly, attachment is not love in any way. As long as the mind is encumbered with possessiveness, jealousy, fear, insecurity, there is no possibility of love whatsoever. Most of us merely use one another to escape utter darkness and emptiness within. We should, then, ask ourselves if using one another is what we want to call love, because that is what we have done so far.

One day, a great scholar was invited to a house of affluents and he was supposed to sleep over as well. However, it was most uncomfortable for him to sleep when a newborn, in a room next to his, started crying all of a sudden in the middle of the night. He was extremely irritated, couldn't bear it up any more, and rushed to the room the wailing was coming from. Lights were on, the baby had his parents sitting by him in bed, tears rolling down their eyes. The scholar was told that the newborn was suffering from a chronic disease that got him feverish almost every night. Great compassion arose in his heart, caressing and consoling the one suffering. His irritation and anger turned into compassion and care and affection, only out of understanding.

Someone has beautifully said, "Take away all that is not love, and that which remains at the end is but love." Let us take away jealousy, fear, possessiveness, attachment, insecurity, and all the other kinds of chaos, and that which remains is only love. The chaos comes out of selfishness, running after something while running away from something else, but there is love and oneness when all self movements come to an end.

If one is seeing a bird flying in the sky, one is not thinking of it, and the moment one starts thinking, one stops seeing, taking oneself away from the bird, into the past. Thought always belongs to the past or the future, but reality is not the past. The past, having got modified, has become the present, and the present, getting modified right before us, is becoming the future. So all the three times are in the Now and they are inseparable. One can see what is before one only when the mind is silent, when one observes both thoughts and the objects outside. Then there remains no duality at all, and the observer themself becomes the objects being observed. In this seeing and oneness, there is understanding, and this understanding is the flower of love.

It's only understanding, then, which is timeless and selfless, that we can call love. This is, of course, a state of the mind, where the lover is the beloved, where both the lover and the beloved are one. This love is the existence of that flower whose fragrance is for every passer-by, no matter whether they nurture it or not. Thus, it is independent of objects.

Running round the clock, we have no time to see whatever is right before us, let alone understanding or being one, and thus we are loveless and dead. We are empty and fill ourselves with comfort and hope, and there can be no oneness, which is love, if there is no stillness, if we keep moving restlessly. Lack of love, they truly say, is therefore sorrow.

CHAPTER TWENTY-FIVE

LIVE TO THE FULLEST

Life is strange, isn't it? We keep running throughout our whole lives, leaving behind almost everything before us, and the moment we lose what we already have, we finally realize its true value. Rarely do we ever stay by the ones standing by us, when one day we notice them wave us off for the last time.

Time flies, but we never get to realize it. The question is, when there is no destination whatsoever, what is it that we run after? Why is it that we fail to embrace the travellers on our journeys? Why is it that we never look around and make the most of our journeys? The amorous, bright eyes of a toddler, the smiles of our beloveds, the caressing of the ones we put our feet in this world through, the trees dancing to the soothing breeze of a waning twilight, they are all rooted in uncertainty; but they speak far more than we ever get to hear, and they do far more than we ever get to feel.

We look back on our childhoods and innocently wish if we could again get them back. Having lost the innocence we were naturally gifted, we ask ourselves today where we have come. Wherever we have come, certainly, we seem to have come a long way now, and going back is merely a fantasy.

What was there yesterday by us has become the present with a new face, having got a little modified. What is here today is changing night and day as well, absolutely ready to take a new face and be by us in the future. Therefore, nothing is new, nor is there any destruction or creation, creation and destruction being the two sides of the same coin. There seems to be only transformation happening all around, impermanence being the only thing permanent around and within us. It seems we never lost or gained anything, when there is absolutely no end to anything or to anyone. The faces change, but the essence remains the same.

There comes about a point of time in everyone's life where they realize that by being nothing, they are everything, that by going nowhere, they are in touch with the whole world, that by having nothing whatsoever, they have everything.

Don't be dejected, dear

Nothing is eternal over here

Waves are we in this ocean

Bound to subside sooner or later

No longer should you wait

No longer should you wail

Come on! Wipe your tears away

Live this life your way

Believe me, this is your time

You will never get to live again

I realized at a very, very early age that the milkman who knocks at my door every morning is far richer with merely a couple of lacks of rupees every year. With a stable family, joyous mental state, and healthy body with longevity, he undoubtedly is far richer than any lawyer or engineer, with a CTC of crores, incapable of smiling even to the wonders of Nature.

The milkman is lucky that he will die one day, unlike most of us who have never been alive at all to die. Indeed, if there is heaven within, one can live joyously even in hell, but if there is hell within, one can't be joyous with even the most wonderous pleasures of heaven.

Unfortunately, the current generation is different from all previous generations in many ways, and it has our youths being pushed to be a slave to a superficial life as well. We wear dresses not for covering bodies in view of culture or civilization but out of our insecurities about our looks; we spend time at Starbucks not because we like its coffees but because we need our Insta handles to look fancy; we learn the English or French language in Asia to sound erudite, and not because we love it; we hit gyms not because we wish to be fit but because good curves turn us into better commodities.

The more chaotic, insecure and fearful we are, the better the economy of a nation, and satisfaction and joy are not something great for the chains of capitalism that we, being capitalists, are all part of now. Our gains and losses premised upon the chaos within us, most of us get used to being chaotic as we move from our teenage to our late twenties.

We blame society for our mental conditions while being unable to understand a simple, clear fact that the very structure of our society has been put together by us—by the chaos and dissatisfaction within us. It goes without saying that we can be free from anything we build.

CHAPTER TWENTY-SIX

SWAMI SACCHIDANANDA

Having walked for years on a secluded path of spirituality, I reached a crossroad with a couple of amicable strangers in my late teenage — strangers as strange to the world as me then. At first glance, it appeared as if I had met them countless times before, every time in different worldly relationships and different situations. The path thus no longer seemed secluded, or even little traveled by me.

The most jovial and emotionally active at the crossroad was Swami Sachidanand, born Kulbhushan Kodwani, and it seemed that he had long been waiting for me there. The moment I reached, therefore, we embraced and rejoiced over our destiny to walk further together.

I cast my mind back to the day when I first interacted with Swamiji over the phone. After having talked for almost one and a half hours about our past spiritual experiences, he was surprised to find out that he was thrice as old as I was. His grandeur was such that he found himself far happier than he would be had he found me his age, since he iterated that he saw a great scope of spiritual evolution within me in view of the rest of my life. Not only that, little did I know we would become the best friends connecting almost every day, no matter whether I was at work or he was out buying vegetables in the evening.

Swamiji was sure we had known each other for hundreds of years as we mingled naturally and effortlessly. He would reiterate, "Ayush Ji, I have never connected to anyone else on my spiritual journey as I have to you. With everyone else, I have witnessed at least a few differences owing to their religiously, politically, or ideologically conditioned minds." We would often discuss how beginning with the observation of breath for a state of meditation is far more practical for his amateur disciples than directly observing the stream of thoughts itself, though our interactions limited to politics, his personal life, and quantum physics during the last few days of his life.

I remember his indifference to my insistence on his presence on YouTube as I felt the need for the world to listen to the rarest like him. In turn, he would many times express his strong desire to see me speaking to the public — something inexplicably fatherly and rather motherly. His disciples eventually succeeded in getting him to speak on social media platforms and my heart was thus full of gaiety. However, this point of our life is what I may regret forever, as that was when my interaction with him reduced to almost once or twice a month. My inner being still reverberates his words, "Ayush Ji, we would walk a little faster on this path after your PhD." Little did I know then I would be left alone on this known path now.

Interacting with his family members, especially his brother, about whom he would often talk, I can still see him alive. He goes on within each and every individual he has influenced in his life. The waves may rise and subside thousands of times, but the ocean goes on.

CHAPTER TWENTY-SEVEN

My Own Journey

My own journey started at a tender age of merely eleven years, right after my father's demise. Out of immense loneliness, I leaped out of my house in search of the supernatural. That is how most of us are, running after new experiences to avoid the inward boredom and loneliness, and the more experience, the closer we are to a point where there is very little to experience in the materialistic world. Only at this point do we start to feel helpless and uncomfortable, and when there remains little in the materialistic world, we begin to look to the supernatural and all that is beyond materialism.

Of course, at such a tender, the materialism of the world rarely mattered to me, and the people around haunted me with cunningness and selfishness. Before looking to the supernatural, as is obvious, I with my loneliness tended to be attached, attachment led to dependence, dependence resulted in the fear of losing, and fear meant more insecurity, jealousy, possessive, and anger, thus leading me to further loneliness. Whatever little intelligence I had soon turned out to be enough for the realization that it was all a vicious loop. The moment I saw the loop as it was, I was free from it.

I found myself professional then, but it seemed to be early to be so—a little early for an eleven-year-old to work as a freelance writer for news agencies, with no real first-hand experience of the crudity and dryness of the corporate-or professional-world. My last resort was my passion and love for books, and within a couple of years, my whole house turned into a handsome library. As I look back, I find out that it started with Gyaan Yoga for me first, followed by Bhakti Yoga.

With very little interest in academics, I befriended my own non-academic books, of history, literature, religion, philosophy, metaphysics, psychology, and so on and so forth. However, since my upbringing had turned me hypersensitive, my loneliness went on, and so did my questions about the life outside and the life within. When loneliness haunted me, I reiterated to myself, "One with none in this world must have the whole universe with one, and no one is thus lonely in this world." I surrendered myself to Mother Nature, and I night and day found myself guided by some intangible power thereafter—Gyaan Yoga, not being enough, was accompanied with Bhakti Yoga, or what you can call 'my surrender'.

Bhakti Yoga brought a level of stillness within my conscious mind, and this readied a fertile ground for the seeds of meditation. I would at times find myself in a state of trance and tranquillity every now and then, sitting on the couch, in bed, walking in parks, travelling, at times even asking myself in a crowd what within me distinguishes me from others around. It was when I realized why I failed to pay attention to lessons in whatever few classes I attended at my primary and secondary schools: moving into different states of consciousness. It never allowed me to perform well at school either.

Bhakti Yoga had led me to Raj Yoga now, that is, the path of meditation, and in some years, I found myself meditative, or aware, during all my activities—reading, speaking, writing, eating, bathing, or walking in a crowd.

As my awareness became deeper and more and more consistent and as the gaps between my thoughts became longer and longer, I found myself in the lore of Karma Yoga as well. This was a realization that Karma Yoga, Gyaan Yoga, Bhakti Yoga, and Raj Yoga are not different but the four faces of awareness itself. Where there is awareness, there must be all the four.

I suggest that you should start wherever your heart finds itself at ease; for Meera and Ramakrishna Paramhamsa, it could be Bhakti, for Swami Vivekananda, it could be Gyaan, for Gautama the Buddha, it could be Dhyaan, and for Krishna, it could be Karma.

My heart wishes you all only joy, since joy is the only purpose of all that you wish for in your life, be it marriage, money, profession, status, or power. Let us be joyous and spread joy all around so that only joy in return could be shared with us as well.